MARY CELESTE

For Alexia, who drifted into our lives.
We will never abandon you.
—Mommy Heidi and Nana Jane

Dedicated with love and gratitude to
my grandmother, Alice Robinson.
—R. R.

First Aladdin Paperbacks edition July 2002
Text copyright © 1999 by Jane Yolen and
Heidi Elisabet Yolen Stemple
Illustrations copyright © 1999 by Roger Roth

ALADDIN PAPERBACKS
An imprint of Simon & Schuster
Children's Publishing Division
1230 Avenue of the Americas
New York, NY 10020

Also available in a Simon & Schuster Books for Young Readers
hardcover edition.
Designed by Paul Zakris
The text of this book was set in 14-point Minister Book.
Printed in Hong Kong
10 9 8 7 6 5 4 3 2 1

The Library of Congress has cataloged the hardcover edition
as follows:
Yolen, Jane.
An unsolved mystery from history: the Mary Celeste / by Jane
Yolen and Heidi Elisabet Yolen Stemple; illustrated by Roger
Roth.
p.   cm.
Summary: A young girl relates the facts that are known about
the unexplained disappearance of the crew on the ship Mary
Celeste in 1872, and challenges the reader to solve the mystery.
ISBN 0-689-81079-2 (hardcover)
[Mary Celeste (Brig)—Fiction.] I. Stemple, Heidi Elisabet
Yolen. II. Roth, Roger, ill. III. Title.
PZ7.Y78Hme   1999
[Fic]—dc21
97-24613
CIP AC
ISBN 0-689-85122-7 (Aladdin pbk.)

A NOTE FROM THE ARTIST:

The illustrations in this book were done in a series of
stages. First I did tiny, rough "thumbnail" sketches.
This is really the fun and creative part for me. Then,
from these thumbnails I made large, detailed pencil
drawings, which I traced onto watercolor paper. Next,
I painted the picture using transparent watercolor,
adding pencil for detail and texture.

ACKNOWLEDGMENTS

The publisher gratefully thanks Mr. Andrew W. German of
the Mystic Seaport Museum for his kind assistance.

BIBLIOGRAPHY

Bradford, Gershom, *The Secret of the Mary Celeste*.
Barre, MA: Barre Publishing Company, 1966.

Bryan, George S., *Mystery Ship: The Mary Celeste in
Fancy and in Fact*. Philadelphia: J. B. Lippincott, (nd).

Cohen, Daniel, *Mysterious Disappearances*. New York:
Dodd, Mead & Company, (nd).

Fay, Charles Edey, *The Story of the Mary Celeste*. New
York: Dover Publications, Inc., 1942.

Harris, John, *Without a Trace*. London: Methuen, 1981.

Lauber, Patricia, *Famous Mysteries of the Sea*. New
York: Thomas Nelson & Sons, 1962.

Lockhart, J. G., *Mysteries of the Sea: A Book of Strange
Tales*. London: Philip Allan & Company, (nd).

THE Mary Celeste

An Unsolved Mystery from History

By Jane Yolen and

Heidi Elisabet Yolen Stemple

Illustrated by Roger Roth

Aladdin Paperbacks

New York London Toronto Sydney Singapore

When I grow up I want to be a detective, just like my dad. He says I was born curious, which is just what a detective needs to be.

What I'm most curious about now is my father's file of old mysteries that have never been solved. They have baffled people for years. Dad calls these cases "open" but I call them "history mysteries," and I am determined to figure them out.

For each mystery, I read as much as I can about it. I keep a notebook in which I highlight the most important clues. Sometimes I draw a map and a time line. And I always keep a list of important words that are special to the case to help me understand what has happened.

The Mary Celeste is about a ship whose crew disappeared when they were on the high seas more than a hundred and twenty years ago. The crew was never found. Though lots of people have ideas—or theories—about what might have happened, no one is sure. But Dad says no mystery is impossible to solve as long as you have enough clues.

This is how the story goes:

A brisk December wind
filled the great sails
of the *Dei Gratia*.
She had left New York
on November 15, 1872,
to cross the cold Atlantic
with a cargo of petroleum.
It was a long trip,
many days on an empty ocean,
and nothing to look at
but the thin line between sea and sky.
Early in the afternoon of December 4
(December 5 in sea time),
seaman John Johnson,
alert at the wheel,
spotted a smudge on the horizon.
He called out excitedly,
"Captain Morehouse, sir,
there is something coming toward us
off the port bow!"

PETROLEUM: crude oil before it has been refined for use

SEAMAN: sailor

SEA TIME: Sea time and shore time are measured twelve hours apart because sea time is counted from noon, when the sun stands directly overhead.

PORT: the left side of a ship (STARBOARD is the right side of a ship)

BOW: the forward part of a ship (STERN is the rear part of a ship)

Dei Gratia is Latin for "By the grace of God." The ship was a Nova Scotian brigantine owned by George F. Miller of Bear River, Nova Scotia. Its captain was David Reed Morehouse.

Captain Morehouse looked through his spyglass.
Even though the smudge was miles away,
he could tell it was a ship
heading in their direction.
But as she came closer,
he saw that the ship moved slowly, oddly,
running aimlessly before the wind.
Only three sails were still set.
Two had been blown away,
and one was lying loose.
The rest of the sails were furled.
Several of the *Dei Gratia*'s crew
gathered at the rail to watch the oncoming brig.
They all knew something was wrong.

When sailors see a ship sailing toward them, they can tell by the way she is moving whether something is wrong. If she "yaws" badly—swinging erratically to the right or left—sailors can easily see there is a problem, even from far away. They can also note if the sails are properly trimmed for the amount of wind that is blowing.

SPYGLASS: a handheld telescope

FURLED: something rolled up or fastened, like a sail

BRIG: short for brigantine, a two-masted ship

"Get me Mr. Deveau," ordered the captain.
A seaman went below deck
to rouse the first mate from his berth.
By the time Deveau joined the captain,
the other ship was near.
"Look!" Morehouse said,
handing the mate the spyglass.
Deveau looked and saw no one on deck.
"But," he said, "they fly no flag of distress.
Perhaps they lie drunken below."
At the wheel, Johnson laughed.
"They wouldn't if they had a captain like ours!"
Captain Morehouse laughed, too, then said,
"Let us hail them."
They ran up the flags that offered help.
Minutes went by and they got no reply.
When they sailed closer still,
the captain called out through his speaking trumpet.
He was greeted by a strange silence.

FIRST MATE: the second-in-command after the captain

BERTH: a sailor's sleeping quarters

HAIL: to call a greeting to a passing ship

SPEAKING TRUMPET: a device like a megaphone used to make a voice louder

MUTINY: when a ship's crew revolts against the captain, usually killing him and taking over the ship

There is an entire alphabet of international signal flags. At that time P over C flown together from the masthead (the top part of the mast) meant "Crew have mutinied."

N over D meant "I must abandon my vessel."

Some people believed the Mary Celeste had a cursed history. She was built in 1860 and originally called Amazon. Her captain, Robert McLellan, took ill and died on her very first voyage. In 1867, she ran ashore in Cape Breton and had to be repaired. In 1868, she was sold to an American and given a new name: Mary Celeste, possibly as a superstitious way to avoid more tragedy.

The Mary Celeste left Pier 44 on New York City's East River on Tuesday, November 5. Because of bad weather, she anchored about a mile "down the harbor"—offshore. As soon as the weather cleared, she set sail again, on November 7, with a light and favorable wind. When next seen—on December 4 (December 5 sea time)—she was 600 miles west of Portugal.

"Something is definitely amiss," the captain said.
"Someone must go over and see."
So a small boat was lowered.
Three of the sailors—
Deveau, Johnson, and second mate John Wright—
rowed across to the silent brig.
The ship was a bit over a hundred feet in length
with an ornamental scroll on her bow.
"What is she called?" asked Johnson.
He was pulling on the oars and so could not see.
"The *Mary Celeste* out of New York," said Deveau,
reading the name on her stern.
The only sounds were their own voices
and the *slip-slap* of the waves.
From the *Mary Celeste* there was silence.

SECOND MATE: the officer
who is next in rank below
the first mate

Deveau and Wright clambered on board,
leaving seaman Johnson behind.
Slowly they searched from bow to stern,
but there was no one up on the deck,
not even at the ship's wheel.
The wheel was neither damaged
nor lashed to a single course.
The lifeboat that should have been lying
across the main hatch was missing.
Wright and Deveau checked the ship's pumps,
which turned out to be in good working order,
and besides there was little water in the hold.
"Mutiny?" whispered Wright,
as if afraid to say the word aloud.
"Or a fever ship?"
"Maybe pirates," Deveau whispered back. "Let's go on."

MAIN HATCH: the largest or most used opening in the deck of a ship

SHIP'S PUMPS: machines for removing excess water in the ship's hold

CELESTE

NEW YORK

FEVER SHIP: a ship on which the crew have all taken ill or died from a disease, perhaps yellow fever or cholera

What would the ship have looked like if the crew had left willingly? Tidy cabins, all navigational aids taken with them, foodstuffs taken as well, the hatches (doors) properly closed, and the wheel tied to a specific course. If pirates had attacked them? Shattered railings, broken doors, smashed cabins indicating fighting, gashes in wood from sword or pistol fights. In fact, when the Mary Celeste's crew disappeared, there were no longer pirates sailing the Atlantic. The last of them had been seen in the 1830s. Mutinies, though rare, had happened as recently as 1857, on the schooner Walter M. Towgood. Deserted or lost ships were not rare. Some recent ones of note: the French ship Rosalie in 1840, the Spanish ship Viego in 1868.

The captain's cabin sat neat and shipshape,
except that the bed had not yet been made—
the print of a small body was on the covers—
and several toys lay scattered on the floor.
An old dress hung near the bed,
some india rubber overshoes standing under it.
In the water closet
sat a bag of dirty clothing.
A rosewood harmonium
stood silent against one wall,
above it a shelf of music books.
The captain of the *Mary Celeste*
had brought his family with him
and many of the comforts of home.
In the first mate's cabin
the ship's log lay open,
the last entry dated 8:00 A.M., November 25th.
No trouble had been noted
up to that time.

WATER CLOSET: the ship's toilet

HARMONIUM: a kind of musical instrument—a reed organ

LOG: the detailed record of a ship's voyage, kept by the first mate

The captain would have been extra careful in choosing the crew with his wife and baby daughter aboard. That crew consisted of first mate Albert Richardson, second mate Andrew Gilling, steward and cook Edward William Head, and four German seamen, two of them brothers, seven in total. They all had reputations as first-class sailors. Mrs. Briggs wrote to her mother that the captain thought the crew "a pretty peaceable set this time all around, if they continue as they have begun. Can't tell yet how smart they are."

Deveau checked the ship's galley—the kitchen—and found all the kettles, pots, and utensils washed up. There was a barrel of flour about two-thirds full. No cooked food was visible. The hold had enough food for the crew for at least six months, including meat and potatoes. It looked as if nothing was out of place or had been taken. "I found," Deveau later testified in court, "no wine, beer, or spirits whatever in the ship."

But some important items were missing from the *Mary Celeste*.
"Where is the chronometer?" asked Wright.
Deveau added, "And where are the sextant, navigation book, and ship's register?"
They both knew a ship would never sail without these.
Had the captain taken them with him when he left?
Then why had the family not taken their clothes
or the captain's wife her jewelry?
The two men asked themselves these questions.
There was nothing to eat or drink in the captain's cabin,
so the sailors checked in the ship's galley and pantry.
There they found a six-month supply
of uncooked food and fresh water.
They checked the crew's quarters,
which were in good order,
except that there was no crew anywhere to be found.

The last place the men looked
was in the ship's hold
where her cargo—
1,700 barrels of raw alcohol—
was well stowed.
Not a single barrel had been opened.
All in all, Deveau and Wright
looked around the *Mary Celeste*
for over half an hour.
They found no sign of anyone on board,
no signs of struggle.

The cargo was alcohol stored in red oak barrels. Red oak is a porous wood that lets alcohol fumes escape. When the barrels were examined, some of the alcohol was found to be gone, but that was entirely due to evaporation. According to reports, the barrels were "in good order" and not "in any way injured." Besides, the alcohol was raw alcohol which was to be used in fortifying Italian wines. Anyone drinking it unprocessed would not become drunk, but would rather lapse into a coma or die. Only one hatch was found open, but there was no sign of smoke damage or an explosion in the unventilated hold.

HOLD: the area inside the ship where cargo is stored

CARGO: the goods being transported by the ship

Captain Benjamin Spooner Briggs was an experienced sailor, who "bore the highest character for seamanship and honesty," according to the United States Consul in Gibraltar. He was born in Wareham, Massachusetts, in 1835, the second of five sons of Captain Nathan Briggs, all of whom but one became sailors. They followed their father's strict rule: no grog—drinking liquor—aboard ship. Captain Benjamin Briggs was a Bible reader and at 27 had married his childhood sweetheart, Sarah Cobb. They spent their honeymoon on board a ship he commanded. When they sailed on the Mary Celeste, they left behind their son Arthur, age seven, who was starting school. Sophia Matilda, age two, came with them.

The men did not speak as they rowed back,
but once on board the *Dei Gratia*,
they had much to say.
The captain listened sadly to their report,
for he knew Captain Briggs and his wife, Sarah.
He had even had dinner with them
at the Astor House before they sailed.
They had told him
their two-year-old daughter, Sophia,
was traveling with them,
but their seven-year-old son, Arthur,
had been left behind to go to school.
Captain Morehouse knew that Captain Briggs
was a good sailor, a smart master, and fair to his crew.
"The men's oilskins, boots, and pipes were all left behind.
The lady left her gold lockets.
They went quickly, sir," said Deveau.
"I do not think they meant to be gone for good."
Then he added: "I propose we bring
the *Mary Celeste* in for salvage.
Now, by the laws of the sea,
she belongs to us."

OILSKINS: rain gear consisting
of a waterproof coat, pants,
and—sometimes—a hat

SALVAGE: rescue of a wrecked
or damaged ship or its cargo

CANADA

NOVA SCOTIA

NEW YORK,
NEW YORK

UNITED STATES

November 4
*Captain Briggs and Captain
Morehouse dine together in New York*

November 5
*Mary Celeste leaves New
York port in bad weather*

November 5-7
*Mary Celeste at anchor
about 1 mile offshore*

November 7
*Mary Celeste sets sail;
wind light and favorable*

November 15
*Dei Gratia sets sail
from New York port*

N

W   E

S

CONTINENT OF
EUROPE

November 25
**Final log entry of the Mary Celeste
says the ship was 6 miles from the
island of Santa Maria**

PORTUGAL

SPAIN

AZORES
(Nine islands belonging
to Portugal)

December 4
Dei Gratia sailors spy the
Mary Celeste **600 miles
west of Portugal**

GIBRALTAR

MADEIRA

CANARY ISLANDS

CONTINENT OF
AFRICA

BAROMETER: an instrument used to determine the air's pressure and the weather

SEAWORTHY: in a fit state for sea voyage

MASTS: long upright poles attached to a ship's deck that support the sails

Captain Morehouse thought about salvaging the boat.
"It will be dangerous for both ships.
Our crew is small.
I cannot spare more than three men."
Deveau nodded. "I can manage, sir," he said.
Deveau took only two sailors,
a small boat, a barometer, a compass, and a watch
and rowed back across to the silent ship.
It took them several days
to make the *Mary Celeste* seaworthy again,
pumping out the small amount of water and
fixing the sails and masts.
Then they sailed her to Gibraltar
where Captain Morehouse and his crew
had to defend their rights to the ship
at a long and difficult salvage trial.
That trial was big news,
reported in all the penny papers of the day.

PENNY PAPERS: the old name for tabloid newspapers because long ago they sold for a penny

The barrels of alcohol were worth $37,000. The ship carried insurance on the freight of $3,400. The ship itself was insured for $14,000. Morehouse expected that he and his crew would get about half that amount for bringing the ship into port. Salvage money is payment from the insurers and the owners of the freight, who are—in a way— buying back the ship and cargo from those who found the derelict. They actually got only a fifth, and out of it had to pay all court costs.

The newsboys on the streets
called out the latest gossip.
"Bloody sword found on *Mary Celeste*!"
"Planks in splinters from a fight!"
"Half-eaten breakfast still on the table!"
"Thirteen missing from cursed ship!"
Readers thrilled to these stories,
but some were half-truths
and some were downright lies.
The only people who knew
what really happened on the *Mary Celeste*,
after the last log entry had been written,
were the ten people on board.
They could have told the real story
if they had ever been found.

They never were.

The "yellow journals," like the tabloids today, sometimes made up stories instead of just reporting actual facts. Some said the ship's cat was asleep when Deveau found him. (There was no cat.) Some said the food was still warm on the stove. (The ship's log indicated people had been last aboard November 25, ten days earlier.) Some said the captain's watch was still ticking on a nail. (This would have been a daily windup watch.) Some said that the ship carried thirteen people, a cursed number. (There were ten, including the captain and his wife and child.) Such details make for better gossip, better stories, but they are simply not true.

So what **DID** happen?

My dad says no one knows for sure.

But now that you have read the story, and have studied my notes, map, time line, and word lists, maybe you can solve the mystery of the *Mary Celeste*. Perhaps you will think one of the old theories is how things really happened. Or maybe you'll come up with a theory of your own.

Only remember, as my dad always says, *Check Your Clues.*

1. The Pirate Theory:

The *Mary Celeste* was set upon by pirates and the crew was murdered or put overboard in the lifeboat.

Were there any signs of a fight?
What valuables were missing?
What valuables remained on the ship?
What was more valuable than the ship itself?

2. The Drunken Crew Theory:

The crew of the *Mary Celeste* got drunk and killed the captain and his family. Then they fled in the lifeboat.

What kind of a man was Captain Briggs?
What kind of alcohol was aboard?
Was any alcohol missing?
What valuables were gone?
Why didn't the crew keep the ship?

3. The Frightened Crew Theory:

The captain and crew were frightened by smoke and fumes escaping from the alcohol. They waited in the lifeboat to see if the *Mary Celeste* was going to explode. For reasons unknown, they were never able to return to the ship.

Was there evidence of smoke and fumes?
What kind of sailor was Captain Briggs?
Were the hatches blown?
Was there evidence of fire on board?

4. The Weather Theories:

Bad weather, whirlpools—even icebergs—were said to have damaged the *Mary Celeste* or frightened the crew into abandoning ship.

What did the ship's log say about weather?

What kind of a sailor was Captain Briggs?

Was the ship damaged?

5. The Sea Monster Theory:

A hundred years ago, there were still people who believed that a sea monster—like a kraken or giant octopus—had somehow devoured the crew.

Is there any creditable biological evidence of sea serpents or sea monsters?

Were there marks of any such struggle on the ship?

6. The DEI GRATIA Conspiracy Theory:

Captain Morehouse and his crew, the only eyewitnesses to the mystery scene, had more to do with the disappearance than they were telling. Perhaps they were the ones who had disposed of the *Mary Celeste*'s crew. Or perhaps Captain Morehouse had conspired with Captain Briggs over dinner the night before the *Mary Celeste* sailed, planning the abandonment.

What family did Captain Briggs leave behind?

What kind of money would have been involved?

How respectable were the two captains?

Those are the six most popular explanations ever given. Are any of them right? Nobody knows for sure. Not the police, not the lawyers, not the reporters, not the historians, and not even my dad. It is a mystery still waiting to be solved. It is, as my dad says, an open file.

But I've got my own theory about what happened to the *Mary Celeste's* crew. And maybe—now—you do, too.